MISS MARY REPORTING

THE TRUE STORY OF SPORTSWRITER MARY GARBER

Written by Sue Macy · Illustrated by C. F. Payne

A PAULA WISEMAN BOOK
SIMON & SCHUSTER BOOKS FOR YOUNG READERS
New York London Toronto Sydney New Delhi

SIMON & SCHUSTER BOOKS FOR YOUNG READERS · An imprint of Simon & Schuster Children's Publishing Division
1230 Avenue of the Americas, New York, New York 10020 · Text copyright © 2016 by Sue Macy · Illustrations copyright © 2016 by C. F. Payne
The Simon & Schuster Speakers Bureau can bring authors to your live event. For more information or to book an event, contact the Simon & Schuster Speakers Bureau
at 1-866-248-3049 or visit our website at www.simonspeakers.com.
Book design by Lucy Ruth Cummins · The text for this book is set in Stempel Garamond. · The illustrations for this book are rendered in mixed media.
Manufactured in China · 1115 SCP · 10 9 8 7 6 5 4 3 2 1 · Library of Congress Cataloging-in-Publication Data
Macy, Sue. · Miss Mary reporting: the true story of sportswriter Mary Garber / Sue Macy ; illustrated by C. F. Payne. · pages cm.
ISBN 978-1-4814-0120-3 (hardcover) · ISBN 978-1-4814-0121-0 (eBook) 1. Garber, Mary, 1916–2008—Juvenile literature. 2. Women sportswriters—United States—
Biography—Juvenile literature. I. Payne, C. F., illustrator. II. Title. · GV742.42.G347M34 2014 · 070.4'49796092—dc23 · [B] · 2014000871

For Ally and Nikki Mack,
future pioneers—S M

For my friends and family
for the continued support
—C.F.P.

$\mathcal{M}$ary Garber was a tiny bit of a girl, but that didn't stop her from playing football with the boys. Tackle football. Over rough and rocky ground. She called her team the Buena Vista Devils (or the BVDs), and of course, she was the quarterback.

It seemed that Mary was born loving sports. Her younger sister, Neely, thought their father helped to feed Mary's interest. "Not having a son, he'd take us to football games and other things," she said. As they watched, he taught his daughters the rules. "He felt if you were a spectator, you ought to know what you were spectating," Neely said.

When she wasn't playing or watching sports, Mary was reading all she could about them. She followed boxing and baseball and loved the football team from the University of Notre Dame in Indiana. But Mary's mother wasn't as patient with her sports-loving daughter as her husband was. Neely said Mrs. Garber believed "that a girl ought to behave like a girl."

Not that Mary's behavior surprised her mom. She was used to her middle daughter's independent streak. When Mary was eight years old, her family moved from New Jersey to North Carolina. Mrs. Garber insisted that her three girls write letters to their grandparents back in the Garden State. Mary's older sister, Helen, did as she was told. So did Neely. But Mary thought letters were boring. So she created a newspaper.

In the *Garber News*, Mary reported all the news and drama from her neighborhood just outside of Winston-Salem: School was closed for the summer. Neely stepped on a tack. The BVDs won another game. The family poodle was run over by a car but escaped injury by crouching in a rut in the bumpy road.

Writing the *Garber News* came naturally to Mary. Early on she set her sights on a career as a newspaper reporter. But opportunities were scarce when she graduated from college. She finally took a job as a society reporter for the *Twin City Sentinel*, a paper in Winston-Salem. Society reporters wrote about parties and other social events. They had to describe the glamorous clothing people wore. That was not at all Mary's cup of tea.

At one dance, Mary remembered, "I got the wrong dress on the wrong lady." After that she brought along a friend who worked at a clothing store to help.

Mary got her big break when the United States entered World War II. Many of the nation's young men joined the armed forces, leaving women to take over their jobs on the home front. After the *Sentinel*'s last sportswriter joined the navy in 1944, the editor put Mary in charge. She kept the sports pages filled until the war was over.

It wasn't easy, especially at the beginning. When Mary went to cover her first college football game, she found that there were no programs identifying the players. How could she describe the action if she didn't know who was making the plays? "I was just desperate," she later remembered. "I didn't know what I was going to do." Fortunately, a spectator saw her helpless expression and volunteered to sit with her and tell her who was who.

"I couldn't have done it if it hadn't been for him," she said. "He really saved my skin."

World War II came to an end, and Mary's boss moved her to the news desk. But a year later she went back to sports for good, just in time to witness an important milestone in baseball. In 1947 the Brooklyn Dodgers added infielder Jackie Robinson to their roster. Back then African-American athletes like Jackie played baseball in the segregated Negro leagues. When he joined the Dodgers, Jackie became the first black player in the major leagues since the 1880s.

In August 1947, Mary traveled to Brooklyn, New York, to watch the first-place Dodgers play three games against the Boston Braves. She was particularly impressed by Jackie's skill at bunting—tapping the ball lightly— for a base hit.

"Last Wednesday he laid down a perfect bunt along the third-base line," she told her readers, "and when Boston pitcher Johnny Sain threw wild to first, Robinson legged it all the way around to third."

Jackie became a role model for Mary. She was inspired by his quiet dignity in the face of taunts and jeers from people who couldn't accept a black man in the major leagues.

"There's no getting around the fact that Robinson met these challenging days with maturity and courage," she would write in 1956. "It takes guts to keep your mouth shut and walk away. It is against every normal reaction of human behavior. But Robinson did it."

Mary had to endure her own share of slights and struggles. The trouble started in the press box, the area of a stadium or arena where reporters watch sports events. In the 1940s women were banned from the press box at college football games. Mary was forced to sit with the coaches' wives until her editor complained. Even after she was allowed in, Mary had to wear the football writers' official press badge, which proclaimed, "Press Box: Women and Children Not Admitted."

Locker rooms posed another problem. After a game, male reporters headed into the teams' locker rooms to interview players while they were changing into their street clothes. But Mary had to wait outside. By the time the players came out to talk to her, the male reporters had rushed back to write their stories. The players also wanted to go home, making it hard for Mary to get good quotes. A few skipped out on her altogether.

Sometimes being a female sports reporter brought unusual requests. For example, a high school basketball coach once asked Mary to sew up a tear in a young man's uniform. Although she was far from a whiz with a needle and thread, Mary agreed to give it a try. "I nearly died during that game," she said, "because every time that kid went up for a rebound I thought, 'Oh, gosh. Those pants are going to rip and his pants are going to fall down and I'm going to be really embarrassed.' But I'm proud to say that they held."

Mary did her job with steady determination. Soon readers looked forward to her bylines. Coaches started to know her and respect her, and young athletes were eager to talk to her.

When Mary started working for the *Sentinel*, many schools in the South were segregated. White children went to all-white schools and black children went to all-black schools. The newspaper rarely covered games at Winston-Salem's all-black schools. But Mary changed that. "It seemed to me that black parents were as interested in what their kids were doing as white parents were," she said. Before long, black athletes were watching for her, hoping she would show up to write about their games.

Mary showed up for more than fifty years. She wrote about baseball, football, basketball, tennis, track and field, and just about every other competitive contest, including marbles. She officially retired in 1986, at age seventy, but after that she kept coming to work every day and writing at least three articles a week. By the time Mary gave up this daily grind in 2002, people realized what an extraordinary career she'd had. She won awards and was voted into the sportswriters' halls of fame.

These honors were part of Mary's legacy as a sportswriter. But so were her encounters with people she'd written about years before. Time after time these adults showed Mary folded, yellowed newspaper clips with her byline that they'd been carrying in their wallets for decades. Mary understood why her reporting had a lasting impact. "I tried whenever I wrote about kids to be as positive as I could," she said. "If you can give a kid a pat on the back or if you can tell him he's done well or you can make him believe in himself, you can make a difference in his life."

Mary also made a difference in the lives of the women who followed in her footsteps. Ashley McGeachy Fox, who covers the National Football League for ESPN.com, was an eight-year-old tennis player in Winston-Salem when Mary wrote an article about her. Years later Mary was her role model as Ashley pursued her own career as a sportswriter. Ashley said, "I remember thinking, if this petite lady in granny glasses can stand up to an angry coach, why can't I?"

According to Mary, the greatest compliment she ever got came from a young boy. It happened in the 1950s when Mary was covering the Soap Box Derby in Winston-Salem. A friend of hers who was sitting in the stands overheard a conversation between two African-American boys about eight and ten years old. The older boy pointed to Mary and asked, "Do you see that lady down there on the field?" The second boy nodded.

"That's Miss Mary Garber. And she doesn't care who you are, or where you're from, or what you are. If you do something, she's going to write about you."

AUTHOR'S NOTE

Mary Garber, reporting from the press box in the 1940s.

Courtesy of the Forsyth Public Library Photograph Collection

MARY GARBER DIDN'T SET OUT TO CHANGE THE WORLD, but change it she did. By reporting on athletic events at black high schools and colleges, she helped bring equality to the sports sections of mainstream southern newspapers, and by extension, to the newspapers themselves. And merely by doing her job, she jump-started the efforts of female sports reporters to gain equal footing with males. Mary often gave credit to her sister, Neely, for making it possible for her to live her dream. Mary resided with Neely in their childhood home until the last year of her life. Neely kept things running on the home front after their father died in the 1950s and their mother in the 1980s.

Newspapers were in their heyday when Mary was covering sports. She started decades before the Internet made instantaneous scores and highlights available, as they are today. Fans might find some local sports news on the radio or TV. But they depended on their hometown papers for write-ups of every local contest, along with photographs and athlete profiles.

Despite retiring when she was seventy, Mary continued to write for the *Winston-Salem Journal* regularly until she was eighty-six years old. She stopped only when her eyesight and hearing began to fail. But sports were the center of her life right to the end. During her final months a minister asked Mary what she hoped would be her "spiritual reward in heaven." She immediately had an answer: "Football season."

ACKNOWLEDGMENTS

On some levels it was easy for me to understand where Mary Garber was coming from. After all, she was a sports lover, like me, and a writer, also like me. But Mary grew up and worked in North Carolina, and that was unfamiliar ground for me. So I headed to Winston-Salem to get to know Mary and her surroundings. Fortunately, that city is the home of the Forsyth County Public Library and its wonderful North Carolina Room. That archive is under the direction of librarian Fambrough "Fam" Brownlee, a fount of local history knowledge. Fam was a wonderful guide and a valued witness, as he played high school sports when he was young and knew Miss Mary. I thank Fam and his colleagues for all their help.

I also thank the folks at Paula Wiseman Books, especially my brilliant editor, Sylvie Frank, who immediately shared my enthusiasm for Mary Garber's story and expertly shepherded this work through the publishing process. Thanks as well to C. F. Payne for his evocative, compelling illustrations. And finally, thanks to my family and friends for indulging my obsession with Miss Mary and encouraging me as I wrote this book.

—S. M.

TIME LINE

1916 Mary Ellen Garber is born on April 16 (some sources say April 19) to Mason and Grace Dean Archer Garber in New York City.

1924 The Garber family moves from Ridgewood, New Jersey, to Winston-Salem, North Carolina.

1938 Mary graduates from Hollins College, a women's school in Roanoke, Virginia, with a degree in philosophy.

1940 Mary begins her job as a society reporter for the *Twin City Sentinel*.

1944 She moves to the sports department until World War II ends in 1945.

1946 Mary becomes a permanent member of the sports department.

1947 She travels to Ebbets Field in Brooklyn, New York, to see Jackie Robinson play.

1976 The National Collegiate Athletic Association (NCAA) changes its rules to allow male and female reporters equal access to locker rooms.

1985 When the *Twin City Sentinel* goes out of business, Mary joins the staff of its sister paper, the *Winston-Salem Journal*.

1986 At her "retirement" party on September 30, Mary declares, "Thanks for the lovely dinner, but I have to be at work early tomorrow, so let's wrap this up."

1989 Winston-Salem holds the first annual Mary Garber Holiday Tip-Off Classic, a girls' high school basketball tournament.

1990 The Atlantic Coast Conference (ACC) of the NCAA establishes the Mary Garber Award to honor the female athlete of the year.

1991 Mary's older sister, Helen Brown, dies.

1996 Mary is elected to the North Carolina Sports Hall of Fame.

1998 She receives an honorary doctorate from the historically black school Winston-Salem State University for her pioneering coverage of their sports program.

2002 Mary writes her last article for the *Winston-Salem Journal*.

2005 She becomes the first woman to win the Associated Press Sports Editors' Red Smith Award.

2006 The Association for Women in Sports Media renames its highest honor, given annually to a trailblazing female sportswriter, the Mary Garber Pioneer Award.

2007 On October 24, Mary's younger sister, Cornelia (Neely), dies at age eighty-six.

2008 In May, Mary is inducted into the Hall of Fame of the National Sportscasters and Sportswriters Association. On September 21 she dies at age ninety-two.

RESOURCES FOR ALL AGES

On the Web

"Oral Histories: Mary Garber"
http://c-spanvideo.org/event/194349
Mary tells her story in this two-hour oral history done by Diane Gentry for the Washington Press Club Foundation's Women in Journalism oral history project in 1990.

"Mary Garber—Pioneer Female Sportswriter—My Tribute," by Clarence Gaines
http://cgscoutperspective.blogspot.com/2011/03/mary-garber-pioneer-female-sportswriter.html
After Mary died, the son of Winston-Salem State's legendary basketball coach "Big House" Gaines wrote this tribute to his father's great friend.

On Film

Nine for IX: *Let Them Wear Towels*, directed by Annie Sundberg and Ricki Stern (ESPN Films, July 16, 2013)
This documentary from ESPN's series of films by and about women focuses on the generation of female reporters after Mary Garber who covered men's sports and fought for greater access and acceptance.

Books

Playing Ball with the Boys: The Rise of Women in the World of Men's Sports, by Betsy M. Ross (Clerisy Press, 2010)
One of the first female anchors at ESPN looks at how women have become part of all aspects of sports, from the broadcast booth to the boardroom to the playing field, with a nod to Mary Garber and other pioneer sportswriters.

A Kind of Grace: A Treasury of Sportswriting by Women, by Ron Rapoport (Zenobia Press, 1994)
Mary Garber wrote the afterword in this collection, which is full of articles and profiles penned by dozens of female sportswriters.

SOURCES

To get the full flavor of Mary Garber's writing, I pored over microfilm issues of the *Twin City Sentinel* and the *Winston-Salem Journal*.

Here are the sources used for the quotations in this book:

Crothers, Tim. "Miss Mary's History Lesson." *Sports Illustrated*, March 20, 2000.

_____. "She's a Sports Pioneer, Too." Associated Press Sports Editors. May 7, 2008. http://archive.apsportseditors.org/news/2008/050708garber_nao.html.

Garber, Mary. "Dodgers Draw Their Fans from All over the Nation." *Twin City Sentinel*, August 18, 1947.

_____. Interview by Diane Gentry. Washington Press Club Foundation. "Women in Journalism." November 4, 1990. http://www.wpcf.org/mary-garber.

_____. "Skirt-in Sports: Jackie Robinson—Symbol." *Twin City Sentinel*, December 15, 1956.

James, Sheryl. "The Dean." *Greensboro News and Record*, November 16, 1986.

Oberle, Terry. "For Her Spiritual Reward? 'Football season,' She Said." *Winston-Salem Journal*, September 22, 2008.

Rawlings, Lenox. "Mary Garber: That Lady in the Press Box Ran Steady and Crossed Some Hurdles to Get There." *Winston-Salem Journal*, September 21, 1986.

NOTES

Here are the sources of specific quotes:

"Not having a son . . . you were spectating": Rawlings, *Winston-Salem Journal*.
"that a girl . . . like a girl": Rawlings, *Winston-Salem Journal*.
"I got . . . wrong lady": James, *Greensboro News & Record*.
"I was just desperate . . . saved my skin": Gentry interview.
"Last Wednesday . . . around to third": Garber, *Twin City Sentinel*, August 18, 1947.
"There's no getting . . . Robinson did it": Garber, *Twin City Sentinel*, December 15, 1956.
"I nearly died . . . that they held": Gentry interview.
"It seemed to me . . . white parents were": Gentry interview.
"I tried whenever . . . in his life": Gentry interview.
"I remember . . . why can't I?": Crothers, *Sports Illustrated*.
"Do you see . . . write about you": Gentry interview.
Author's Note:
"spiritual reward . . . Football season": Oberle, *Winston-Salem Journal*.
Timeline:
"Thanks for . . . wrap this up": Oberle, *Winston-Salem Journal*.